The
WHOLE
RELATIONSHIPS
WORKBOOK

Guided Exercises for
Whole Love and
Healthy Relationships

by

Annette R. Purkiss

allwrite
publishing

Atlanta, GA

The Whole Relationships Workbook: Guided Exercises for Whole Love and Healthy Relationships
Copyright © 2026

For more info, contact the publisher at:

Allwrite Publishing
1445 Woodmont Lane NW #495
Atlanta, GA 30318
info@allwritepublishing.com

ISBN: 978-1-941716-47-2 (paperback)
ISBN: 978-1-941716-49-6 (ebook)

Printed in the United States of America

CONTENTS

WELCOME & HOW TO USE THIS WORKBOOK

Welcome, you're in the right place to begin the work of wholeness.

I wrote this workbook because I learned the hard way: **wholeness begins within**. This is a gentle, practical start to building a Whole Relationship, one where two imperfect people practice self-awareness, surrender, and mutual service.

The full book, "**Whole Relationships: How Imperfect People Create Unbroken Love**," provides the deeper teaching, detail, and frameworks that anchor what you will begin here. This workbook is designed to help you actively practice and apply what the book reveals.

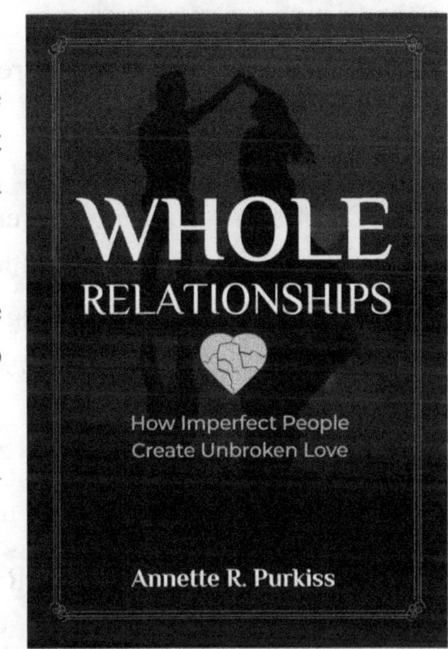

If you find yourself wanting more clarity, context, or guidance as you move through these exercises, the book will help you understand not just what to do, but why it matters and how to sustain it.

What you'll do here:

1. Identify where you are now

2. Recognize what your soul truly needs

3. Begin practicing whole love today

Before we begin, take a moment to pause. Then complete the sentence below.

Right now, what I desire most in my relationships is:

PART I — BEGINNING THE JOURNEY

INTRODUCTION

This workbook was created to accompany *Whole Relationships*, but it can also be used on its own as a guided reflection tool. While the book explains the ideas behind wholeness in relationships, this workbook helps you **practice them**. Through short reflections, prompts, and exercises, you'll explore the essential dimensions of whole love:

• **ARC of Self** — building awareness, respect, and confidence within (*Who am I being in relationships?*)
• **Soul Needs** — recognizing what your heart and soul truly require (*Why do I respond the way I do?*)
• **TORCH of Love** — practicing trust, openness, respect, communication, and humility in relationships (*How do whole people love each other?*)

The Whole Relationships Path

Whole love grows through four movements:

1. **See yourself clearly** (ARC)

2. **Understand your soul needs and acknowledging others'**

3. **Practice whole love with others** (TORCH)

4. **Commit to relationship from wholeness**

You don't need to complete this workbook perfectly or in order. The goal is not performance but **honesty and awareness**.

Throughout the workbook, you'll see a set of visual guides placed at intentional moments:

Wholeness Pause — a moment to <u>pause & reflect</u> and let something settle	
Reflection Moment — an invitation for <u>journaling</u> or quiet thought	
Discernment Marker — a gentle signal to <u>proceed slowly</u> and thoughtfully	

Wholeness grows through small moments of truth. Take your time. Write freely. Return often.

WHAT IS A WHOLE RELATIONSHIP?

A Whole Relationship involves two imperfect, perhaps broken people, who are self-aware, surrendered, and servants to each other's soul needs.

- **Self-aware** → **ARC of Self** (Awareness, Respect, Confidence)

- **Surrendered** → **TORCH of Love** (Trust, Openness, Respect, Communication, Humility)

- **Servanthood** → **Soul Needs** (Universal: Truth, Faith, Love; Unique: Talent, Traits, Time)

Quick Reflection

1. Which word speaks most to you right now?

   ☐ Self-aware

   ☐ Surrendered

   ☐ Servant-hearted

2. What does "wholeness" mean for you in this season?

Wholeness Reminder: Healing reduces pain. Wholeness integrates truth. This workbook focuses on living whole, not revisiting every wound.

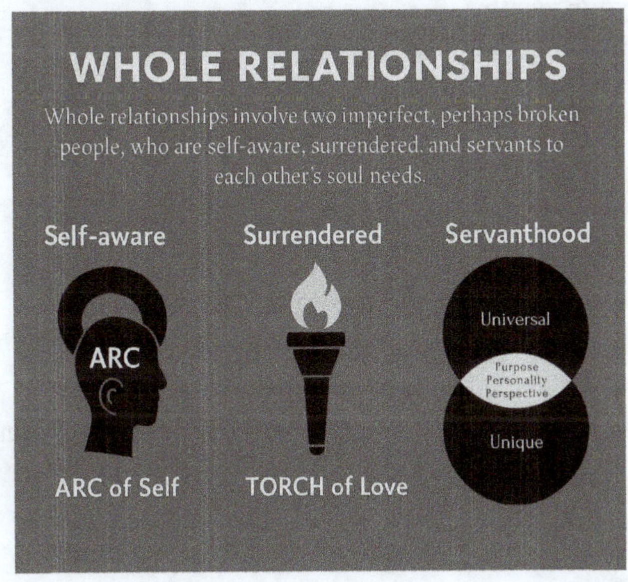

PART ll — THE ARC OF SELF

ARC OF SELF REFLECTION

You can't love whole until you live whole. The first step is **self-awareness, the soul's mirror.**

A.R.C. = Awareness • Respect • Confidence

Self-Awareness — See clearly

What patterns keep repeating in your relationships (dating, friendship, family, work)?

- Pattern #1 ____
- Pattern #2 ____
- Trigger I notice most: _______________________________________

Self-Respect — Honor your boundaries

- A boundary I've struggled to uphold is: ____________________
- The truth this boundary protects is: ____________________

Self-Confidence — Stand in your worth
Write 3 affirmations that feel true enough to practice daily:

1. I am ____
2. I deserve ____
3. I choose ____

 ***Wholeness Tip:*** Forgive yourself for what you did to survive. Honor yourself now that you're healing.

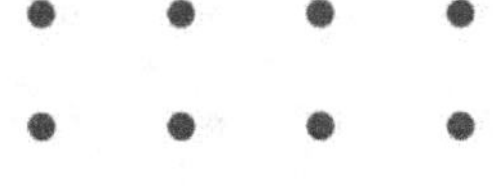

ARC OF SELF PRACTICE

When Protection Becomes a Pattern

Many of us protect love in different ways. Some pull away to feel safe. Some try harder to hold the connection together.

These strategies once served a purpose, but over time, they can quietly cost us intimacy, clarity, and self-respect.

Gentle Pattern Check-In (Circle what resonates)

When relationships feel uncertain, I tend to:

☐ Create distance or withdraw
☐ Stay busy, distracted, or emotionally numb
☐ Try harder, give more, or over-explain
☐ Manage the relationship to keep it stable
☐ Shut down instead of speaking honestly

Wholeness reminder: This is not a diagnosis. It's awareness.

Micro-Choice Practice (Choose ONE)

Today, instead of defaulting to protection, I will practice one small act of wholeness:

☐ Pause before withdrawing
☐ Name one need without justifying it
☐ Allow silence without rushing to fix it
☐ Stop over-explaining and speak simply
☐ Take space without disappearing

Write it in your own words:

This week, I choose to ____.

Important Boundary (recommended)

o   Awareness is the beginning, not the burden.

o   Some patterns require support beyond reflection.

o   Seeking help is not failure; it is self-respect.

Rapid Inventory (circle all that apply):

- I pause before reacting: **Never • Sometimes • Often • Always**

- I say what I need without apologizing for the need itself: **Never • Sometimes • Often • Always**

- I keep one small promise to myself daily: **Never • Sometimes • Often • Always**

Boundary Script (fill-in)

"For me to feel safe/respected, I need ____________________.

When ____________________ happens, I will ____________________.

If that boundary isn't honored, I will ____________________."

Confidence Builder (evidence list)

Three things I did well this month:

1. ____

2. ____

3. ____

Language Check

Notice how you speak about yourself. Is your inner language rooted in shame and survival or truth and alignment?

Rewrite one sentence you often think about yourself using whole language instead of broken language.

ARC Checkpoint

What new awareness have you discovered about yourself?

CREATING A PERSONAL RULE OF LIFE

Wholeness is not maintained by insight alone. It is sustained through daily choices that protect alignment over comfort. A **Rule of Life** is not a list of restrictions or a test of discipline. It is a set of personal commitments that create conditions where truth, integrity, and self-respect are easier to live out consistently.

Your Rule of Life is not meant to control you. It is meant to **support your** alignment. It ensures your actions, decisions, and habits are in harmony with your values, purpose, and truth.

It will evolve over time. It should be realistic, compassionate, and aligned with who you are becoming, not who you think you "should" be.

Step 1: Notice the Symptoms

Before setting any rules, begin with awareness of a recurring problem and/or significant behavioral pattern(s) that is causing you to struggle. Reflect on moments where this issue tends to influence your decisions.

Check any patterns that feel familiar or come up with your own:

☐ **Distraction**
Avoiding responsibilities by chasing novelty, validation, stimulation, or busyness

☐ **Delay**
Procrastinating on what you know is important, urgent, or meaningful

☐ **Denial**
Ignoring truths, red flags, or inner wisdom to stay comfortable

☐ **Doubt**
Second-guessing yourself, mistrusting discernment, or relying only on feelings

☐ **Disregulation**
Over-investing energy in one area (work, relationships, projects) while neglecting others

☐ **Dissecting**
Overthinking a circumstance, leading to stress, negativity and/or assumptions

☐ **Impulsivity**
Acting quickly to relieve discomfort, avoid reflection, or regain a sense of control

☐ **Defensiveness**
Resisting feedback, correction, or accountability to protect self-image

☐ **People-Pleasing**
Over-agreeing, over-giving, or self-silencing to avoid conflict or rejection

☐ **Withdrawal**
Pulling away emotionally or relationally when things feel overwhelming

☐ **Other**

____

Reflection:
Which patterns show up most often for you?

When do they tend to appear?

Step 2: Name the Through-Line

Many surface struggles share a deeper, common root. Thus, our objective now is to recognize the common theme or issue that appears in various forms: **the through-line**

Complete one or more of these sentences honestly:

- "When I react instead of respond, I am often protecting ______________________."
- "When I avoid or delay, I am often protecting ______________________."
- "When I become defensive or impulsive, I am often protecting ______________________."
- "When I overextend or people-please, I am often protecting ______________________."

Now complete:

- "When I choose alignment instead of reaction, I am protecting ______________________."
- "When I act with intention rather than habit, I am protecting ______________________."

This tension is not a flaw. It is information. Your Rule of Life exists to support alignment at this exact pressure point.

Step 3: Set a Supportive Rule

There are slightly different kinds of rules depending on the circumstance. Orientation rules, for instance, help you begin your day aligned rather than reactive. They re-orient you to your values, grounding your attitude and outlook.

What Life Rules Can Look Like

A Rule of Life is not a personality overhaul. It is usually **simple, specific, and supportive**. Below are examples of personal life rules different people might choose, depending on their patterns. These are **illustrations**, not expectations.

Examples of Orientation Rules

- *Truth before comfort*
- *Faith before feelings*
- *Pause before reacting*

Examples of Decision Filters

- "What am I trying to avoid right now?"
- "If I weren't afraid, what would I choose?"
- "Is this aligned with who I want to be tomorrow?"

Examples of Regulation Rules

- Step away before speaking when offended.
- Write before reacting.
- Move the body before making decisions.

Important: Your rules should meet *your* patterns within *your* reality.
A rule that feels punitive will not last, but a rule that feels supportive will.

Your turn:

My Orientation Rule:
(How do I want to begin my day or respond important moments?)

"Before I respond, decide or engage, I will ___________________________________."

Step 4: Create One Decision Filter

Decision filters help you pause before defaulting to avoidance or impulse.

Example:
If fear or comfort weren't leading, what would faith do next?

My Decision Filter:
(One question I can ask myself when stuck or avoiding)

"Before I delay or distract, I will ask: ___________________________________."

Step 5: Develop a Regulation Rule

Regulation rules **prioritize proactive regulation over reactive stress management**.

Example:
When I'm feeling anxious or agitated, I will take a deep breath and even ask for a timeout if necessary before responding to someone I love or value.

My Regulation Rule:
(What is something I can do immediately to regulate my nervous system?)

"Before I react, I will do this: _______________________________________ to clear my thoughts and remind myself that I am (feeling) _____________________ but still safe."

Step 6: Establish One Boundary

Boundaries protect your energy and attention.

Choose **one** simple boundary that feels supportive, not punishing.

My Whole Love Boundary:

Examples of Distraction Boundaries

- No new tasks before touching one existing responsibility

- No responding when emotionally activated

- Five minutes of progress counts

"Before I _______________________, I will _______________________."

Step 7: Review Practice

Always review your efforts to create and execute your life rules.

Examples of Review Practices

- Review alignment, not outcomes

- Name one moment of courage daily

- Notice where integrity was chosen over ease

At the end of the day or week, answer one or two of these questions:

- Where did I act in alignment, even when it felt uncomfortable?

- Where did I choose comfort, and what was I protecting?

- What is one small moment of growth I can acknowledge?

 **Reminder**

You are reviewing **adherence and alignment**, not outcomes or perfection. You will not follow your Rule of Life perfectly. This is practice, so breaking a rule is not failure; it's feedback. Consistency, not intensity, is what retrains awareness, respect and confidence over time.

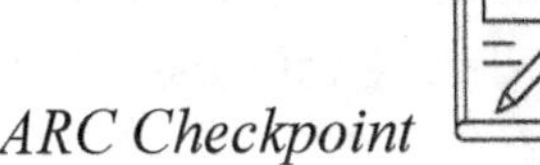

ARC Checkpoint

What one small boundary could change your relational life?

PART III — WHOLE HEALING

FIVE L'S OF WHOLE HEALING

Whole healing is not about forgetting what happened. It's about how what happened is held, interpreted, and lived with over time. The Five L's are not requirements, steps or stages. They are invitations to whole healing. You may return to one repeatedly, skip another entirely, or discover them in a different order. Wholeness honors your pace.

To move through trauma, brokenness, or significant life disruption, you will eventually need to *find a way* to engage each of these movements, gently and honestly.

LAUGH at the situation

Find the funny

Laughter can be a powerful form of release. It does not deny pain, but it softens its grip. As many comedians have discovered, finding humor in what once hurt can create emotional distance from shame and help you realize you are not alone in your experience. Laughter reminds you that pain does not get the final word.

Reflection: What feels heavy right now that you might one day be able to hold with lightness?

LEARN from the situation

Find the wisdom

Some lessons can only be learned by going through difficulty. Over time, painful experiences often reveal insight, discernment, or clarity that reshapes how you see yourself and others. Learning does not mean justifying harm. It means allowing wisdom to emerge so the same wound does not repeat itself in different forms.

Reflection: What has this experience taught you about yourself, your needs, or your boundaries?

LOVE in spite of the situation

Find the release (without minimizing harm)

Love here does not mean reconciliation, excusing behavior, or returning to unsafe situations. It means releasing the grip of resentment so it no longer defines you. Forgiveness begins with extending grace to yourself, especially for what you did to survive. When possible and appropriate, it may also include releasing others from the role of villain in your story, without denying the truth of what occurred.

Reflection: Where might holding on be costing you more than letting go?

LIVE anew because of the situation

Find new meaning

Some experiences change us permanently. They alter our priorities, identities or environments. Living anew means allowing life to look different without interpreting that difference as loss alone. It is the willingness to step into a future shaped by growth rather than fear, even when it doesn't resemble what you once imagined.

Reflection: What feels newly important to you now that wasn't before?

LAUNCH purpose from the situation

Find the purpose

Not everyone is called to start a program or organization, but many are called to offer wisdom, compassion, or guidance born from experience. Some of the most impactful movements, support systems, and ministries were created by people who transformed personal pain into shared purpose. Launching may look like mentoring, advocating, creating, or simply showing up differently for others.

Reflection: How might your experience help someone else feel less alone?

The Goal of the Five L's

The goal is not productivity, positivity, or public success. The goal is **freedom**.

- o Freedom from being defined by what happened.

- o Freedom to live with integrity and meaning.

- o Freedom to experience wholeness without denying your story.

Whole-Life Reminder

- Laughter is good for the **soul**.

- Learning is good for the **mind**.

- Love is good for the **heart**.

- Living anew is good for the **body**.

- Launching purpose is good for the **spirit**, both yours and others'.

THE LENS OF HEALING PRACTICE

Healing is not only about what you confront. It is also about how you *choose to see* it. Sometimes growth is not found in intensity, but in gentle reframing. The 5 L's invite you to shift your perspective in a way that softens resistance and opens the door to wholeness, restoring alignment.

This does not mean dismissing pain or abandoning your values. It means learning how to meet your life with a posture that heals rather than hardens.

The Lens

- **Look for the laugh** → *Lightness*
- **Look for the lesson** → *Humility*
- **Look for the love** → *Compassion*
- **Look at the positives** → *Gratitude*
- **Look for the opportunity** → *Optimism*

Exercise: Reframing a Real Moment

Think of a recent situation that felt frustrating, disappointing or heavy.

Briefly describe the situation:

Now, let's refocus the lens:

1. Look for the laugh (Lightness)
What lightness, irony, or small moment of relief can you find here to smile about?

2. Look for the opportunity (Optimism)
What could this situation make possible for you?

3. Look for the lesson (Humility)
What is this experience teaching you about yourself, others, or life?

4. Look at the positives (Gratitude)
What is still good, present, or working in your favor?

5. Look for the love (Compassion)
Where can you extend grace, whether to yourself or someone else?

BALANCE AS A MIRROR OF WHOLENESS

One of the clearest ways to understand where you are in your healing is to look at how your life is balanced. Where your time, energy, and attention go often reveals what is being honored and what is being neglected. This section is designed to help you see those patterns clearly.

Using the major life areas of Heart, Home, Health, and Hustle, you will begin to notice where you may be overinvested and where you may be undernourished. The goal is not to judge yourself, but to recognize where realignment is needed.

As you move through this exercise, pay attention to what feels full, what feels empty, and what feels ignored. Awareness is the first step toward healing, and balance is one of its clearest reflections.

The Four Areas of a Whole Life

Wholeness is not lived in one area of life. It is expressed across the parts that sustain you daily. To help you see and steward your life more clearly, this workbook is organized around four essential areas:

- **Heart** (connection / commitment)
Your relationships and emotional world. This includes how you give and receive love, the quality of your connections, and the care you extend to others and yourself.

- **Home** (maintenance and/or repair)
The systems and environment that support your life. This includes your home, responsibilities, finances, and the practical upkeep that creates order and stability.

- **Health** (body and energy)
Your physical well-being and capacity. This includes movement, rest, nourishment, and how you care for your body so you can sustain the life you are building.

- **Hustle** (purpose and progress)
Your work, calling, and meaningful output. This includes the focused effort you give to what you've been called to build, create, or contribute.

No single area defines your life. When one consistently dominates or is neglected, imbalance begins to form. Wholeness is not about equal time, but intentional attention.

<u>Reflection</u>: **Where is my life asking for more care and where have I been giving too much?**

DAILY BALANCE: WHOLE LIFE FORMULA

Awareness reveals where your life is out of balance, but awareness alone does not create change. Wholeness is not just something you recognize; it is something you practice.

The structure that follows is not about perfection or pressure. It is a way to gently realign your daily life so that what matters is not consistently neglected. As you move through it, remember: the goal is not to do everything, but to honor each part of your life with intention.

Mindset Shifts:

- **Discipline is spiritual.** Discipline is not just a habit; it's a daily alignment with your higher purpose. For instance, it's your soul saying "yes" to growth even when your body and mind say "no."
- **Focus is warfare.** Every distraction is an attack. Every notification, every mental detour is the enemy. Winning focus is winning the battle for your future.

1. Command the Day Before It Commands You

- **Win the first hour of every day.** Your morning sets the tone for the entire day. Own it.
- **Wake up at the same time every day.** Consistency creates momentum. A disciplined start trains your brain for decisive action.
- **Establish internal order before external input.** No phone, email, or social media until your mind is calm, centered, and ready. Begin with clarity, not chaos.

2. Set Nonnegotiable Outcomes

- **Don't just fill your day with tasks, define progress.** Choose three (3) key outcomes that truly move your life forward, not just keep you busy. (When you really feel overwhelmed, just one key, mission-critical outcome may be enough.)
- **Use this powerful filter:**
  "If I only accomplished these three things today, would the day still matter? " If the answer is yes, you're focused. If not, you're just active.

3. Time Block with Aggression

- **Put your top three outcomes directly into your calendar.** Don't leave them to chance or find "spare time." Schedule them like appointments with your future.
- **Protect these blocks like your life depends on them because it does.** These hours *are* your future. If you don't fight for them, no one will.
- **Refuse to end the day until the big three are done.** This is your contract with yourself. Completion over comfort.

DAILY WHOLE LIFE WORKSHEET

Win the First Hour

☐ Wake up at the same time
☐ Unplug (no phone, email, or social media)
☐ Quiet grounding (prayer / meditation / journaling / reading)

Bonus – One Small Win in Each Area:

- Heart: _______________________________

- Home: _______________________________

- Health: _______________________________

- Hustle: _______________________________

My 3 Non-Negotiable Outcomes

(Choose one goal in at least three areas. If I complete these, will my day feel meaningful and balanced?)

1. ____

2. ____

3. ____

Time Block Plan

(Schedule your BIG 3+ touchpoints in each quadrant for today. Protect them like appointments.)

- Heart (connection): _______________________________

- Home (maintenance): _______________________________

- Health (movement / rest / meals): _______________________

- Hustle (deep work): _______________________________

☑ Daily Check-In

- Did I love well today? (Heart) ☐ Yes / ☐ No

- Did I maintain my world? (Home) ☐ Yes / ☐ No

- Did I care for my body and energy? (Health) ☐ Yes / ☐ No

- Did I push forward what matters most? (Hustle) ☐ Yes / ☐ No

PART IV — SOUL NEEDS

UNDERSTANDING YOUR SOUL NEEDS

Your soul has two types of needs:

Universal Needs (for all of us): Truth • Faith • Love

Unique Needs (by design): Talent • Traits • Time

Your soul needs are sacred, not selfish.

Identify (write one for each):

- A universal need that feels unmet: _________________________________

- A unique need I've been neglecting (talent/trait/time): _________________________

Reflect

- Where might I be using something temporary to fill a permanent soul need?

Pray/Journal

- "God, help me release _________________ and receive _________________ with peace."

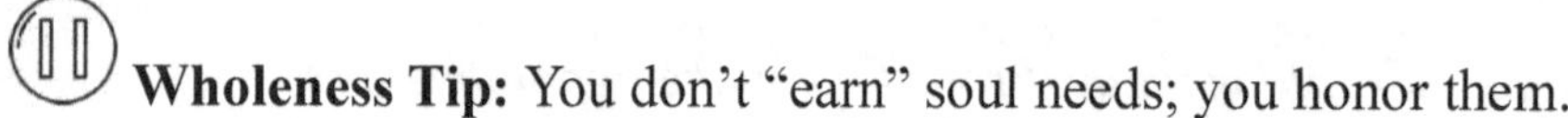 **Wholeness Tip:** You don't "earn" soul needs; you honor them.

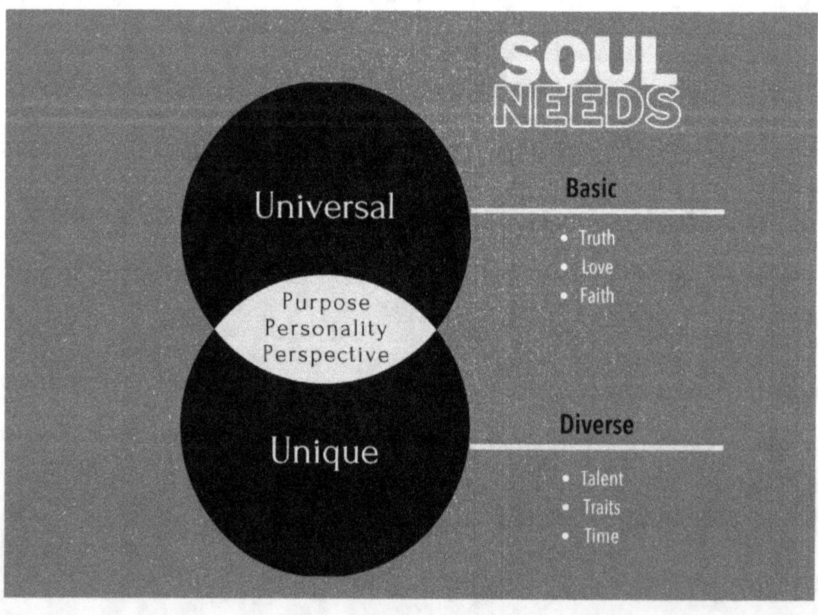

YOUR SOUL'S UNIQUE SHAPE

We don't all need the same things in the same way. What nourishes one person may drain another. Your soul needs arise where **who you are** meets **how you live**.

Your Shape at a Glance (PPP)

This is not about labeling yourself. It's about noticing patterns.

Purpose — *What feels meaningful to you*

Which statements resonate most?

☐ Creating, expressing, or innovating
☐ Serving, supporting, or caring for others
☐ Building, leading, or organizing
☐ Learning, understanding, or exploring

Personality — *How you engage with the world*

When you feel most yourself, do you tend to need:

☐ Solitude and reflection
☐ One-on-one depth
☐ Group energy and interaction
☐ Structure and predictability

Perspective — *How you make sense of life*

You tend to feel grounded when you are connected to:

☐ Spiritual meaning or faith
☐ Logic, knowledge, or understanding
☐ Justice, fairness, or ethics
☐ Beauty, creativity, or harmony

Note: There are no right answers. Only honest ones.

Soul Needs Reflection

1. Which universal need feels most neglected: **Truth, Love, or Faith**?

2. Name two **unique needs** that come from your purpose/personality/perspective (**PPP**).

3. Identify which talent/traits/time (**TTT**) resource each requires.

4. Translate each need into a **clear request** and **one boundary** that protects it.

SOUL NEEDS PRACTICE

Zero-Tolerance Promises to Myself

- I will tell the **truth** even when it costs me comfort. Initial: ___

- I will prioritize **faith** over fear-driven urgency. Initial: ___

- I will give and receive **love** without bargaining for my worth. Initial: ___

Unique Needs Map

- **Talent I must use more:** _______________________________

- **Trait I must protect (e.g., sensitivity, focus):** _______________

- **Time I must defend (best hours, Sabbath, deep work):** _______

Partner/People Check

- Who consistently **recognizes** my needs? _________________

- Who consistently **respects** my needs? _________________

Reflection

As I look at my responses, I notice that I often need ___________________ in relationships, and I've sometimes minimized or ignored that.

Remember: Your needs are not excessive. They are shaped by who you are. Wholeness begins when you stop negotiating against your own design.

Your design explains *why* needs arise, and wholeness determines *how* they are expressed. Soul intelligence gives you the wisdom to *respond* to that clarity with love, empathy, humility, and alignment. Essentially, Soul Intelligence is childlike clarity applied with adult wisdom.

Childlike Expression Practice

1. **Recall a recent conflict.** What would the childlike version of your need have said in one sentence?

2. **Translate it to adult practice** (add specificity and respect).

3. **Name the TLF need** at the core (Truth, Love, or Faith).

4. **Name one TTT resource** it relies on (Talent, Trait, or Time).

5. **Make a childlike request** you can ask for this week.

STAGES OF SERVING SOUL NEEDS

You are not meant to move through all stages of serving your soul needs at once. These stages describe *where attention is forming*, not how well you are doing.

Read each description slowly and notice which one reflects your current experience most honestly. Choose one.

Stages

Acknowledgement — "I know it."
☐ I'm beginning to recognize a soul need I've ignored, minimized, or misunderstood.
☐ I can name it, but I don't yet know what to do with it.

Analysis — "I examine it."
☐ I'm thinking about why this need exists and how it has shown up over time.
☐ I'm connecting patterns, beliefs, or past experiences to this need.

Actualization — "I feel the effects of it."
☐ I'm noticing how honoring or neglecting this need affects my energy, emotions, or relationships.
☐ I'm experiencing clarity or discomfort as this need becomes more real.

Attainment — "I pursue what aligns with it."
☐ I'm making choices that support this need consistently.
☐ My actions reflect alignment, not just awareness.

Discernment Layer

Discernment — "I choose wisely, consistently, and maturely."

Discernment does not rush you forward. It asks whether your current focus is appropriate for this season.

Reflection (choose one):

☐ The stage I'm in feels right for me right now.

☐ I've been trying to move ahead before this stage is integrated.

☐ I'm learning to let one stage be enough.

Growth does not come from acceleration. It comes from alignment.

PART V — THE TORCH OF LOVE

TORCH OF LOVE REFLECTION

Whole love burns brightest when fueled by humility.

T.O.R.C.H. = Trust • Openness • Respect • Communication • Humility

Finish the lines in your own voice:

- **Trust:** "You can rely on me because ___________________."

- **Openness:** "When I'm honest about my feelings, I notice __________."

- **Respect:** "I show respect by _____________________."

- **Communication:** "Good communication looks like ____________."

- **Humility:** "When I'm wrong, I ________________________."

Wholeness Tip: Whole love doesn't compete or control; it listens and learns.

Tools:

An I-message or I-statement is *a form of interpersonal communication* in which people express their feelings, beliefs, or values from the first-person (I, me or my). As such, they start off with "I feel" or "I need" to express emotions and needs directly without blaming, accusing, or triggering defensiveness in others.

Example of I-Message:

Instead of "You're too loud," try: "I'm having trouble focusing on my work right now with the volume at that level."

You start by recognizing the emotion you're experiencing and then taking responsibility for your reaction or state of mind. Try to compose an I-message to counter the you-statements below:

You never *listen.*	_______________________________
You made me *mad.*	_______________________________
You let *me down.*	_______________________________
You are always *late.*	_______________________________
You (your own)	_______________________________

TORCH OF LOVE PRACTICE

Reliability Check (4 weeks)

Each week, choose one small promise you'll keep to someone you love.

- Week 1 Promise: _________________ Result: ____________
- Week 2 Promise: _________________ Result: ____________
- Week 3 Promise: _________________ Result: ____________
- Week 4 Promise: _________________ Result: ____________

Your Trust Audit

- Do I keep my word even when it's inconvenient?
- Do I create safety or suspicion with my communication style?
- Am I reliable or am I controlling?
- Can my loved ones relax in my presence?

Openness Sentence Stems

- "I feel _________ when _________ because _________."
- "I want _________ and I'm willing to _________."
- "I don't want _________ and I need _________ instead."

Practicing Clear, Humble Communication

Sentence Starters:

- "I feel _______ when _______ because _______."
- "What I need right now is ___________."
- "I may be wrong, but my experience is _________."

Repair Language

- "I see how that affected you."
- "Here's what I'll do differently next time."
- "Thank you for telling me the truth."

Repair Script (Humility):

"I'm sorry for ___________. I understand it made you feel _________.
Here's what I'll do differently next time: _____________________.
Is there anything more you need to feel whole with me?"

PHASES OF LOVE REFLECTION

Love does not begin with commitment. It begins with feeling.

Many people move too quickly, not because they are wrong, but because they misname what they feel. What feels like love is often attraction, curiosity or emotional comfort.

Each phase of love reveals something, not just about the other person, but about you.

This section is not about labeling your relationship. It is about recognizing where you are, so you can respond with clarity instead of assumption.

✦ Phase 1 — Attraction

"I feel drawn to you."

Attraction is the initial pull. It may be physical, emotional, or spiritual. It carries energy, excitement, and possibility, but it does not yet reveal compatibility or alignment.

Reflection

- What specifically draws me to this person?

- Am I observing clearly, or interpreting quickly?

Check-In

☐ I am allowing myself to feel without assigning meaning
☐ I am assuming this connection is deeper than it is

✦ Phase 2 — Interest

"I want to know more."

Interest moves beyond the spark into curiosity. You begin to engage, ask questions, and explore who the person actually is.

Reflection

- Am I genuinely interested in who this person is?

- Or am I responding to how they appear or present themselves?

Check-In

☐ I am staying curious and present
☐ I am projecting potential instead of noticing reality

✦ Phase 3 — Like

"I enjoy you."

Liking is comfort. You enjoy the person's presence, conversation, and shared moments. There is ease, but ease does not equal depth.

Reflection

- Do I enjoy this person, or do I feel attached to the idea of them?

- Is this connection consistent, or situational?

Check-In

☐ I am enjoying the connection without over-investing
☐ I am beginning to expect more than has been established

✦ Phase 4 — Admiration

"I value you."

Admiration shifts the focus from how the person makes you feel to who they actually are. It includes respect for their character, values, or consistency.

Reflection

- What do I genuinely respect about this person?

- Do I value who they are, or how they make me feel?

Check-In

☐ I respect this person's character and choices
☐ I am more drawn to the feeling than the person

✦ Phase 5 — Love

"I choose you."

Love is both feeling and decision. It is grounded in truth, not illusion. It allows for imperfection while remaining aligned in values, growth, and mutual care.

Reflection

- Is what I feel grounded in truth, or driven by fear or need?

- Am I choosing this person clearly?

Check-In

☐ My connection is rooted in clarity and alignment
☐ My connection is driven by attachment, fear, or urgency

✦ Pattern Awareness

Skipping phases creates confusion.

When we move too quickly:

- Attraction gets labeled as love.

- Interest becomes assumed commitment.

- Comfort becomes mistaken for alignment.

Reflection

- Where have I moved too quickly in the past?

- What did I assume that wasn't yet true?

✦ Integration

Each phase answers a different question:

- Attraction → *Am I drawn to you?*

- Interest → *Do I want to know you?*

- Like → *Do I enjoy being with you?*

- Admiration → *Do I value who you are?*

- Love → *Can we build something aligned together?*

Practice

Where am I right now in this relationship?

What would it look like to honor this phase without rushing ahead?

PART VI — ASSESSMENT & INTEGRATION

WHOLE RELATIONSHIP QUICK SELF-ASSESSMENT

Circle 1–4 for each (1 = Not true of me, 3 = Neutral, 5 = Very true of me)

ARC (Self-Awareness)

1. I reflect before I react.   1 2 3 4 5
2. I uphold healthy boundaries.   1 2 3 4 5
3. I speak my needs clearly.   1 2 3 4 5
4. I keep small promises to myself.   1 2 3 4 5

Soul Needs (Servanthood)

5. I can name my top universal need this season.   1 2 3 4 5
6. I honor a unique need (talent/trait/time) weekly.   1 2 3 4 5
7. I can tell when I'm "stuffing" a soul need with a substitute.   1 2 3 4 5
8. I can ask for what truly nourishes me without guilt.   1 2 3 4 5

TORCH (Surrender in Relationship)

9. People experience me as reliable.   1 2 3 4 5
10. I share feelings and desires honestly.   1 2 3 4 5
11. I practice respectful communication under stress.   1 2 3 4 5
12. I apologize well and repair quickly.   1 2 3 4 5

Add your total and see what the result means in Part VII. This exercise is educational, not clinical.

TOTAL________

Next Steps:

To determine what your score currently suggests, go to **page 40** for the assessment scoring results.

Join the Wholeness Circle on Facebook

www.facebook.com/groups/wholerelationships/

Reflection & Next Steps

What stood out most to you?

Which one needs attention now?

☐ ARC (Self-Awareness)
☐ Soul Needs (Servanthood)
☐ TORCH (Surrender)

One small step I'll take in the next 48 hours:

PRACTICES THAT BUILD WHOLENESS

These are practices that develop wholeness:

- **Name the reach:** "Right now, I'm asking this person to define my worth. I release that job."

- **Boundary rewrite:** Convert any rule you have for others into a boundary for you. ("Don't call me after 10" → "I don't answer after 10.")

- **Truth swap:** Replace a lie you live by with language that liberates. ("I'm too much" → "I'm divinely made; I'll be met where I'm cherished.")

- **Soul need check-in:** What universal need (truth, love, faith) is hungry? What unique need (talent, traits, time) needs expression this week?

- **TORCH audit:** Did I show up today as reliable, open, honoring, clear, and humble? Where do I need repair?

Wholeness grows through small daily choices. For the next 30 days, choose one simple practice to repeat. Examples include:

☐ Pause before reacting in emotionally charged moments
☐ Speak one honest need each day
☐ Keep one small promise to yourself daily
☐ Reflect each evening on where you chose truth over comfort
☐ Practice gratitude for one relationship in your life

MY 30-DAY WHOLENESS PRACTICE

Daily Check-In

Check off each day that you attempt a wholeness practice. Include notes (i.e. observations or feedback) about your efforts or effectiveness.

Day 1 ☐ _______________________	Day 16 ☐ _______________________
Day 2 ☐ _______________________	Day 17 ☐ _______________________
Day 3 ☐ _______________________	Day 18 ☐ _______________________
Day 4 ☐ _______________________	Day 19 ☐ _______________________
Day 5 ☐ _______________________	Day 20 ☐ _______________________
Day 6 ☐ _______________________	Day 21 ☐ _______________________
Day 7 ☐ _______________________	Day 22 ☐ _______________________
Day 8 ☐ _______________________	Day 23 ☐ _______________________
Day 9 ☐ _______________________	Day 24 ☐ _______________________
Day 10 ☐ _______________________	Day 25 ☐ _______________________
Day 11 ☐ _______________________	Day 26 ☐ _______________________
Day 12 ☐ _______________________	Day 27 ☐ _______________________
Day 13 ☐ _______________________	Day 28 ☐ _______________________
Day 14 ☐ _______________________	Day 29 ☐ _______________________
Day 15 ☐ _______________________	Day 30 ☐ _______________________

Wholeness Checkpoint

What changed in me during these 30 days?

What became easier?

What did I learn about myself?

YOUR WHOLE RELATIONSHIP PLAN

A "Whole Relationship" is not just healthier, kinder, or more compatible. It runs on a different operating system. Most relationships organize around need, performance or control. A whole relationship organizes around truth, alignment, and mutual stewardship of each other's soul.

1. Three things I now understand about myself:

1.

2.

3.

One truth I must no longer ignore:

One soul need I must honor:

2. Alignment Commitments (How I Will Live)

One relationship pattern I will change:

One boundary I will establish or strengthen:

One whole love practice I will commit to this month:

3. Whole Relationship Check-In

For those pursuing or involved with someone, what phase of love are you in?

Are both you and your partner prepared for the next phase?

If not, what is creating misalignment?

(Check all that apply)

☐ Lack of clarity
☐ Unmet needs
☐ Emotional inconsistency
☐ Different expectations
☐ Avoidance of truth
☐ Other: _______________________

✦ Integration Reflection

What conversation needs to happen next?

If I am not in a relationship:

What kind of relationship am I now prepared to sustain?

4. TORCH Check: The State of Our Connection

Evaluate your current (or desired) relationship using TORCH:

Trust
Do I feel emotionally safe, secure, and consistent in this connection?
→ Where is trust strong? Where is it strained?

Openness
Can we be honest without fear of rejection, shutdown, or retaliation?
→ What am I not saying that needs to be said?

Respect
Are boundaries, values, and individuality honored on both sides?
→ Where do I feel honored? Where do I feel diminished?

Communication
Do we understand each other or just react to each other?
→ What patterns keep repeating in how we talk?

Humility
Are we both willing to grow, take accountability, and adjust?
→ Where is pride blocking progress?

5. The Whole Relationship Standard (Your Filter)

I will no longer accept relationships that require me to:

____

____

I will intentionally cultivate relationships that:

____

____

6. Whole Relationship Rhythms

In a whole relationship, we commit to:

- **Regular truth-telling** (not waiting until things break)
- **Checking in on each other's needs** (not assuming)
- **Addressing tension early** (not storing resentment)
- **Maintaining individual alignment** (not losing ourselves)
- **Growing together, not just staying together**

✦ Final Integration Questions

What is one rhythm I will practice consistently in my relationships to protect wholeness?

Is this a relationship where wholeness can be sustained or only pursued?

7. Whole Life Alignment Checck

Where am I currently out of alignment (too much vs. too little)?

- **Heart** (connection):
- **Home** (maintenance):
- **Health** (body/energy care):
- **Hustle** (work/purpose):

Which area needs the most immediate attention and why?

What is one small, realistic shift I will make this week?

Declaration of Wholeness

"I am committed to becoming a whole person, not a perfect one."

"I will pursue relationships that reflect truth, growth, and mutual care."

"I will no longer abandon myself to be accepted."

"I choose wholeness in how I live, how I love, and how I show up."

PART VII — SPIRITUAL PRACTICES

Rooting Wholeness in Truth, Love and Faith

Wholeness is not sustained by effort alone. It is strengthened by what you return to consistently. As such, these reflections are not meant to be rushed. Sit with them. Return to them. Let them guide you.

✦ Reflection 1 — Awareness

"Search me, O God, and know my heart; try me, and know my thoughts…" (Psalm 139:23-24)

Reflection:

- What is God revealing about me right now?

- What have I been avoiding that needs honesty?

✦ Reflection 2 — Alignment

"Above all else, guard your heart…" (Proverbs 4:23)

Reflection:

- What am I allowing that disrupts my peace or clarity?

- Where do I need stronger boundaries?

✦ Reflection 3 — Love through Faith

"… faith working through love" (Galatians 5:6)

Reflection:

- How am I showing up in love right now?

- Where do I need to grow in humility, patience or truth?

DEVOTIONAL REFLECTION

Rooting Wholeness in Truth, Love and Faith

Wholeness is not sustained by effort alone. It is strengthened by what you return to consistently.

This 3-day devotional is designed to help you slow down, reflect, and realign. Take one day at a time. Read the scripture, sit with it, and respond honestly.

You may write your response, pray, or simply reflect.

Day 1 — Romans 12:2 (Mind renewal)

"Do not conform to the pattern of this world, but be transformed by the renewing of your mind...

**Reflection**

Where is God inviting me to think differently about love, relationships, or myself?

Day 2 — Psalm 139:14 (Worth)

"I praise you because I am fearfully and wonderfully made..."

**Reflection**

What about me have I minimized or overlooked that reflects my value?

Day 3 — 1 Corinthians 13:4–7 (Love in practice)

"Love is patient, love is kind..."

**Reflection**

Which expression of love (patience, kindness, humility, etc.) do I need to practice intentionally this week?

Return to these reflections whenever you feel unclear, disconnected, or misaligned.

BLESSING THE JOURNEY

You don't need a perfect past to build unbroken love, only a willing heart. May truth, faith, and love guide your steps into wholeness. If this workbook helped you, you may want to explore the rest of the Whole Relationships resources.

Continue Your Journey...

Book: *Whole Relationships* — Read or listen to (audiobook) a sample free online.

Email: Join the **Wholeness Circle** for monthly reflections & tools.

Quiz: Discover more about your Wholeness Type (Whole, Healing or Hiding) on at the website

Course: *Whole Love* mini course or masterclass

Use the QR code to get a discounted copy of the book.

Visit the website for more information and updates:

wholerelationship.com

Need extra practice?
Download the Whole Life Worksheet on our website along with the TORCH techniques graphic

Assessment Scoring Results:

- **46–60** → Whole & Growing
- **31–45** → Healing in Progress
- **24–30** → Hiding or Hurting

Whole & Growing

- I am aware of my patterns and working on them
- I can name my needs without shame
- I take responsibility for my behavior in relationships
- I am learning to love others without losing myself

Healing in Progress

- I see patterns I want to change
- I sometimes struggle with boundaries or honesty
- I am beginning to understand my soul needs
- I want healthier relationships but still feel uncertain how

Hiding or Hurting

- I often avoid conflict or difficult truths
- I struggle to express my needs
- I feel disconnected from myself in relationships
- I often feel misunderstood or unseen